THE WOULD-BE BOURGEOIS (BÜRGER SCHIPPEL)

A Comedy from the Heroic Life of the Middle Class

Carl Sternheim

Translated from the German by

Laurence Senelick

BROADWAY PLAY PUBLISHING INC
New York
www.broadwayplaypublishing.com
info@broadwayplaypublishing.com

Cover art: detail from *The Pillars of Society* by George Grosz, 1926

First edition: March 2023
I S B N: 978-0-88145-973-9

Book design: Marie Donovan
Page make-up: Adobe InDesign
Typeface: Palatino

PREFATORY NOTE

The best plays of Carl Sternheim (1878-1942) are part of a cycle he called *From the Heroic Life of the Middle Class* (*Aus dem bürgerlichen Heldenleben*) The title is a deliberate oxymoron. The heroes of traditional drama are exceptional individuals, often of noble or royal blood. Neoclassic critics relegated the middle class to comedy as its proper sphere. Sternheim promotes it to heroic status because, in a world dominated by capitalism, the bourgeoisie becomes the foremost agent in human relations.

The Romantics had singled out the extraordinary individual, often pitted against society, as the appropriate hero for a literary work. Sternheim subscribes to this with a difference. In a rotten, decadent society, rebirth must come not from collective action or "causes", but from the transformation of the individual. While those around them are stuck in their social roles, the leading characters adapt to circumstances, often by devious and underhanded means.

The salient characteristic of Sternheim's theatre is condensation. The dialogue is rapid and staccato, any lyricism undercut by cynicism. The characters are also condensed, with the psychologies intensified to the point that they move beyond being types or figures and become monstrous caricatures. Their world exists only by means of their personalities.

In an essay "The Bourgeoisie Preserved" (*Das gerettete Bürgertum*), Sternheim declares that each of them "is passionately and heroically willing himself and his primal forces to resist society." They have seen through the hypocrisy of self-styled altruism and ruthlessly aspire to power. Sternheim satirizes mediocrity and philistinism, but those same vices and flaws are exploited by his protagonists to better themselves. They are anti-heroes whose corruption reflects that of the community in which they have to function. Yet Sternheim doesn't necessarily endorse such means and ends. His moral stance keeps shifting from one side to the other, so that his heroes are themselves objects of satire.

Bürger Schippel (written 1911/12, produced 1913), the sixth comedy in Sternheim's cycle, is a prime example of this. When Brecht wrote a caricature of the ascension of Hitler, he called it *The Resistible Rise of Arturo Ui*. Sternheim's play might be titled *The Restistible Rise of Paul Schippel*. The title character achieves his goal not by means of ruthless gangsterism like Ui, but by sudden bursts of metamorphosis. Jolted by the force of circumstance and edified by chance encounters, he grows from a timid outcast to a Nietzschean superman. In the last act, faced with a duel, he seems to revert to his earlier avatar, complaining that conditions imposed from outside compel him to behave "out of character." Nevertheless, when he is at his most abject, bourgeois society misreads his actions in accord with its unyielding code of conduct, so that he ends up, as he had hoped, enrolled into it as Bürger Schippel.

In German usage, a Bürger was originally the resident of a town, particularly a householder. During the Middle Ages the class was awarded certain privileges, such as eligibility for government office. In this respect, it is closer to the English burgher than the

French bourgeois. In France by the 17th century, the bourgeoisie constituted an identifiable middle class whose status derived from its financial influence. In the nineteenth century, it came to dominate French society. In Germany, however, it remained subservient to the hereditary aristocracy and the military castes. It was classified into subspecies. The *Kleinbürger* was the small-town dweller, fond of a quiet, inactive life, harmless and docile. The *Spiessbürger* was more aggressive, a narrow-minded Philistine addicted to creature comforts; his brutal profile frequently appears in the drawings of George Grosz.

In literature, the Bürger, like the bourgeois, is often described as the antithesis of the artist. This is a favorite contrast in Thomas Mann. The Bürger's taste is retrograde with a fondness for *Kitsch*. In the opera *Mahagonny* by Brecht and Weill, one such character sits smoking a cigar in a brothel as he listens to a working girl playing "The Maiden's Prayer" on a tinkling piano. "Ah," he says, puffing away, "that is eternal art."

Sternheim offers a variant of this theme by employing the German glorification of the *Lied* or art-song. A feature of bourgeois German life, brought to North America by immigrants, were *Liederkranz* or Prize Song societies, male vocal groups who competed for crowns and laurel wreaths. Their repertoires were composed both of classical *Lieder* and folksongs found in such popular collections as *Das Knabenwunderhorn* (*The Lad's Magic Horn*), later transfigured by Gustav Mahler.

In Sternheim this distinctly German idolatry of music is a basic component of the comedy. The Prince, at the apex of the society, at first is indifferent to the song contest, but, under Thekla's influence, declares that the German *Lied* goes straight to his heart. The propertied class and civil service, Hicketier and his friends, worship art as a means of self-aggrandizement and social distinction. Schippel, on the other hand, in his own words, "a lousy musician" but a natural-born tenor, capitalizes on his artistic talent to become a Bürger.

In 1972 the British playwright C P Taylor adapted Sternheim's play as *Schippel the Plumber,* a farce which enjoyed great success, particularly after ex-Goon Harry Secombe took the lead in the retitled *The Plumber's Progress.* Making Schippel a plumber, though it offered opportunities for jokes about pipes and water closets, runs entirely counter to Sternheim's intention. Plumbing is a relatively lucrative trade and tradesmen are usually ranked as lower middle-class. Schippel has to begin the play as an outsider, a penniless bastard, the lowest of the low, if his ascension to the bourgeoisie is to make the author's sardonic point. Sternheim makes it clear that his only source of income is as a barroom "flute-tootler," the shabbiest sort of artist; at the same time he is a pro, in contrast to the amateur quartet. It is his vocal talent that gives him the edge in his dealings with his "betters." (Ernst Dóhnanyi entitled his opera based on *Schippel The Tenor.*)

How then to translate the title? Earlier translators had recourse to *Paul Schippel, Esq.* and *Citizen Schippel.* The critic Otto Mann wrote of Sternheim, "He wanted to be a German Molière…In Germany we don't have any other writers of comedy whose comic spirit, like Molière's, has this dark undertone, bordering on the tragic." So it may be appropriate to adopt the Frenchman's satire *Le bourgeois gentilhomme,* known in English as *The Would-be Gentleman,* and dub Schippel *The Would-be Bourgeois.*

Laurence Senelick

For Albert Bassermann, the brilliant actor.[1]

---

1   Albert Bassermann (1867-1952) starred in Sternheim's play *The Snob*.

CHARACTERS

THE PRINCE
TILMANN HICKETIER, *a goldsmith*
JENNY HICKETIER, *his wife*
THEKLA HICKETIER, *his sister*
HEINRICH KREY, *in the* PRINCE*'s civil service*
ANDREAS WOLKE, *owner of a printing works*
PAUL SCHIPPEL
A DOCTOR
MÜLLER *and* SCHULTZE[2]

2   *Production note: The lines and actions of* MÜLLER
and SCHULTZE *can be redistributed to the* DOCTOR *and*
HICKETIER.

ACT ONE

(A middle-class living-room at HICKETIER's)

THEKLA: *(Very pale blond, enters right)* Are you alone, Jenny? At midnight I heard a sound at the back fence, saw a shadow, the shape of a man crouching down.

JENNY: Thekla!

THEKLA: Lurking there for an eternity, while I stared at him. He caught sight of me, didn't move a muscle. At last, to help him out of his plight, I stepped back. He went away. Who could it be?

JENNY: Your latest admirer.

THEKLA: Why act like a thief in the night and then go away?

JENNY: You must've been mistaken. You still haven't recovered from Adolf's death.

THEKLA: Don't bring up Naumann. He was a repulsive creature, even if he was my fiancé. He was so uptight he gave me cramps.

JENNY: Now he rests in peace. The men will be back from the funeral soon. I wonder if they sang "How gently do they lie at rest" —without the dead man's tenor part?

THEKLA: This morning! He's really truly dead and gone. It makes me so happy I'm over my fear of last night's spook.

JENNY: You once thought better of Naumann.

THEKLA: One evening last June settled it. The two of us were alone. I thrilled to the thought of giving myself to him body and soul. If he had said a word, made a sign, I would have thrown myself at him. The nitwit never made a peep. His calf's eyes popping out of his head.

JENNY: Child!

THEKLA: It was over. I was free again.

JENNY: Don't spoil Tilmann's idea of his friend.

THEKLA: Or his idea of my saintliness. In my brother's imagination we shall remain bride and groom on top of a wedding cake. For his sake I play the inconsolable widow.

JENNY: His nature needs symbols.

THEKLA: (*Has removed a golden laurel wreath from a cushion under a glass bell and, laughing, puts it on her head.*) Behold his two highest ideals joined together: his sister and the wreath twice won in the song competition.

JENNY: Which, owing to Naumann's death on the eve of the festival, is in jeopardy.

THEKLA: In hindsight his demise was inconsiderate. But they intend to ask Schippel…

JENNY: There are serious complications where he's concerned. I can't tell you what sort.

THEKLA: I've known for a long time: he's a bastard.

JENNY: You must never let on you know that word when Tilmann's around.

THEKLA: I mustn't even let on I know about the stork when Tilmann's around.

JENNY: The men consider it an abomination. They can't make up their minds to ask him. Meanwhile time's running out. Yesterday the Prince returned to the castle. Tilmann's managed to keep calm, but Wolke and Krey…

THEKLA: *(Laughs)* Are frantic!

JENNY: Laugh if you like. Their sort of men don't have enough romance in them.

THEKLA: Compared to Tilmann they're yahoos.

JENNY: Because you don't care to look at their good points.

THEKLA: If I look at Krey at all he flies into a panic. An eligible girl terrifies the confirmed bachelor.

JENNY: Wolke is fond of you; he's always been fond of you.

THEKLA: Then Krey a thousand times over! He can be trained. *(Suddenly)* Last night's phantom, his bulk, his shape reminded me of Wolke's. Can it be—Wolke bent on a moonlight romance? *(She bursts out laughing.)* If so I might even take a liking to him. For I've never been so feverishly in need of a hero.

JENNY: Child!

THEKLA: *(Draws JENNY's hand to her bosom)* The equinox is upon us. The beginning of summer.

(HICKETIER, KREY and WOLKE enter in frock-coats and top hats.)

HICKETIER: *(To THEKLA)* My poor dear sister!

WOLKE: He departed in glory, so to speak, snatched away in the prime of life. A splendid funeral. Insipid without a tenor, though. Dull. What do you think, Krey?

KREY: *(Quietly)* Shut up!

WOLKE: *(To THEKLA)* In fitting appreciation of your feelings we…how's it go?

HICKETIER: Dear child.

THEKLA: Leave me alone! *(Exits)*

HICKETIER: It was a bolt from the blue.

WOLKE: Shaken her to the core of her being. Our task is to—how's it go? He was, take him for all in all, a man.

KREY: There's no time for idle chatter. Where's the letter, Hicketier?

HICKETIER: I'll get it.

JENNY: Did you write to Schippel?

HICKETIER: *(To* JENNY*)* Stay with Thekla. She's going through a rough patch.

JENNY: Seeing how level-headed she is, she'll get over it.

*(*JENNY *and* HICKETIER *exit.)*

WOLKE: Women's indifference is an enigma. The corpse is barely cold, and his intended is already over him. Perhaps she's got someone else in her sights.

KREY: You and that malicious tongue of yours!

WOLKE: As if I didn't know.

KREY: What's that supposed to mean?

WOLKE: So you've got nothing to tell me?

KREY: Mind your manners!

WOLKE: I know what to think.

HICKETIER: *(Comes back)* The typewriter spared me having to communicate with this lowlife in my own handwriting. A rubber stamp added my name at the end with no "respectfully yours" or "kind regards".

KREY: Given the circumstances that may be a mistake. Read it.

HICKETIER: *(Reads)* Messrs. Hicketier, Krey and Wolke—I put our names in alphabetical order—might be disposed to entrust you with the tenor part in their vocal quartet on a provisional basis. You are instructed to appear on Monday the fourteenth—that's today— at three o'clock in the afternoon at the undersigned's address. Hicketier.

WOLKE: Bravo. To the point.

KREY: Sounds like ordering a dog to obey. The tone of a tax bill.

WOLKE: Is this Schippel, so to speak, that much better than a dog?

KREY: If he's got any backbone, he'll be furious.

HICKETIER: As I wrote it, I was seething with rage at the humiliation of having to make the first move—it was the bloodiest sacrifice of my life.

KREY: You should have come to me for advice. As a government secretary I know all the correspondence styles. There are ways of expressing yourself courteously even when seething with rage. After a note like this the man may ignore us and we'll end up in the soup.

WOLKE: Even so Hicketier will have done his duty.

KREY: Is that enough? We're talking about winning here.

WOLKE: Should he write: we have the honor, yours respectfully, to a foundling?

HICKETIER: So he can boast to the whole town how we sat up and begged?

KREY: Rubbish. If he refuses, we can't sing. Forget about the prize wreath.

WOLKE: In all likelihood—how's it go?

HICKETIER: *(Wiping off sweat)* What a dreadful situation!

WOLKE: I'm at a loss.

KREY: According to experts this fellow's voice surpasses Naumann's. With him we could beat the efforts of any quartet in the whole principality.

WOLKE: So what's your opinion?

KREY: I hardly think any independent-minded person would comply with such a rude invitation.

WOLKE: Oh God, oh God, oh God!

HICKETIER: Independent-minded, a wretched flute-tootler? Our influence with his betters could cost him his livelihood.

(The three sit apart in the three corners of the room and look at one another helplessly.)

HICKETIER *(Sheepishly)* Wolke?

WOLKE: Oh God, oh God! Krey, what do you have to say?

KREY: "Instructed to appear!" Ha!

HICKETIER: I suppose you should have written it! But a Hicketier, goldsmiths whose family business dates back to the Thirty Years War.

WOLKE: The Wolkes are not to be sneezed at either.

KREY: As a senior civil servant am I to prostitute myself? If only you'd have come to me; I have at my disposal a whole arsenal of vapid clichés.

HICKETIER: What next?

WOLKE: This much is clear: we have got to enter the song competition.

KREY: Or give up as men what inspired us as boys.

WOLKE: Madness!

HICKETIER: A legacy from my forebears. What we promised the deceased on his deathbed we must hold sacred.

KREY: So, since the members of a quartet must be native born and local residents, and no other tenor is available, we are…

HICKETIER: At the mercy of this Schippel's favor or disfavor.

WOLKE: And in a situation like this you write a letter like that, Hicketier! I'm sweating blood and water.

HICKETIER: *(In despair)* With my strongest feelings warring within me, I forced myself to do what was humanly possible.

KREY: It wasn't enough to meet our needs.

WOLKE: God help us out of this unholy mess. Amen.

KREY: *(Looks out the window, suddenly)* Schippel!

HICKETIER & WOLKE: *(Together)* Ha!

HICKETIER: Summoned for three o'clock, it's only one. What do you say to that?

KREY: It could mean trouble.

WOLKE: How so? My knees are trembling, Krey, you've got me totally confused.

KREY: Lily-liver! Stand still!

HICKETIER: Who'll do the talking?

KREY: You're master of the house, you "instructed" him.

WOLKE: But be careful. Make allowances.

KREY: Be impressive but unimpressed.

WOLKE: Easy does it!

(PAUL SCHIPPEL, thin, redhaired, around thirty, enters.)

SCHIPPEL: Schippel…Paul Schippel.

HICKETIER: Indeed.

SCHIPPEL: You're Hicketier?

HICKETIER: *(Flares up)* Herr, Herr Hicketier! I must insist.

WOLKE: Psst!

SCHIPPEL: Sorry.

WOLKE: Wolke, proprietor of a printing works and member of the town council. *(Bows)*

KREY: Krey.

HICKETIER: You are…

SCHIPPEL: Play the clarinet. A licorice stick with nickel-plated stops, if you know what I mean.

WOLKE: *(Mimes blowing a flute)* I know, I know.

SCHIPPEL: *(Laughs)* First-rate imitation. I'm a poor man, gentlemen. The dregs of society, as they say in your crowd. The coat on my back is my entire wardrobe. I play very badly.

WOLKE: Rough and ready.

SCHIPPEL: Otherwise I'd be in a good orchestra, not the local beer-hall band. The notes I blow sound desperate, like the trumpet on the Day of Judgement. *(He roars with laughter.)*

HICKETIER: I was unlikely to overestimate you.

SCHIPPEL: Never mind, no opinion of my music-making could be too low. In short, honored sirs: my playing is lousy, as flat as the beer.

WOLKE: *(Roars with laughter)* Very good!

SCHIPPEL: Want to know how much I earn? About twenty marks a week. Meat twice a week, but for the most part rabbit food, on what you might call my salad days.

WOLKE: That's a good one!

SCHIPPEL: Sleep in an attic, no teeth to my comb, no bristles to my toothbrush. Story of my life.

HICKETIER: Revolting details. Your background is well known.

SCHIPPEL: You amaze me, Herr Hicketier.

HICKETIER: A bastard.

(SCHIPPEL *laughs.* WOLKE *laughs.*)

SCHIPPEL: How easily you say it. In these surroundings it never would have made it out of my mouth. But you're so self-confident you broke the ice. So I don't have to mince words; I don't know who my parents were.

KREY: A minor indiscretion.

HICKETIER: Let it rest.

WOLKE: In obscurity.

SCHIPPEL: Sorry, gentlemen, but it's to the point, insofar as my insignificance is the point. We want things to be on the up and up: I'm a bastard, gentlemen. That's a condition you're probably dealing with for the first time.

KREY: But still a common and rather widespread condition.

WOLKE: I sit on the board of an orphanage, so I'm well acquainted with it.

SCHIPPEL: You might almost say a time-honored condition, insofar as…

HICKETIER To be brief, are you willing to sing with us?

SCHIPPEL: Kindly let me have my say. After all, I'm explaining the essence of my insignificance.

KREY: Story of his life.

SCHIPPEL: Don't you notice how I keep my head down?

HICKETIER: I haven't paid you that much attention.

SCHIPPEL: Here's the thing: I don't feel free inside, as a person. And then there's the luxuriousness of this parlor. What I was saying just now I blurted out like in a fever. Please forgive me, I'll be over it in a minute. When I was a kid I'd go up to the other kids in the street to play. Just on the off-chance, of course. They'd kick me. One girl spat in my face. Ever since then I've kept my head down, more familiar with the ground than the sky.

WOLKE: Things like that don't happen nowadays. The foundlings entrusted to my care enjoy all the— how does it go?

SCHIPPEL: Most kind of you. Long story short, I've been rotting in a corner where the sun never shines. Your letter shows up. You must realize how suddenly my situation changes. Ignored, neglected, starved and greedy for whatever comes my way…

HICKETIER: This invitation is your parole from working-class hardship.

SCHIPPEL: You hit the nail on the head. Please understand how confused I feel standing before you. A sudden change for the better, a rebirth, as it were, is taking place.

HICKETIER: That's all to the good, if rather too personal…

SCHIPPEL: (*Walking around the room, stops in front of a picture*) What a wonderful picture! An oil painting, I suppose.

HICKETIER: You will audition today and we shall reach our decision.

(SCHIPPEL *plunges into singing a dazzling A and holds it for a long time.*)

KREY: Oho!

HICKETIER: We can assume from that note…

WOLKE: Bravo!

SCHIPPEL: Yes indeed, my dear sirs, yes indeed, it's going to be magnificent! Incidentally I did have a mother, a kind, decent one.

(SCHIPPEL *takes* HICKETIER *by a button on his coat.*)

HICKETIER: Let go of my coat!

SCHIPPEL: *(Confused)* Meaning no harm.

(SCHIPPEL *holds out his hand to* HICKETIER. *He ignores it.*)

Your hand on it, your hand, Herr Hicketier!

HICKETIER: Ours is strictly a business arrangement.

SCHIPPEL: Your hand, just your hand, I say.

HICKETIER: Ours is a strictly business…

SCHIPPEL: Why not shake hands?

WOLKE: Hicketier!

SCHIPPEL: I'm simply asking—how shall I put it? Firmly but naturally asking for a handshake, a normal greeting at any time. Here, anywhere, your arm, a response, a word on the street, in a tavern, a private house. How about it?

KREY: Your acceptance into the quartet excludes any closer relationships.

SCHIPPEL: Excludes? What's that mean? My voice is singing along with yours—but no handshake?

(SCHIPPEL *violently shakes both of* KREY's *hands.*)

HICKETIER: Are you insane, man?

WOLKE: Oh God, oh God!

KREY: Make him stop!

HICKETIER: That'll do, my good man. Your brain is exploding. Clear it of your delusions and face this bare fact: you, a pauper, may regard us as the providers of your pitiful sustenance, so to speak, with the power to take even that away from you. However, if your voice suits us, we are willing to do something towards better rations, a new coat, even a little coin in your pocket. That is all, and for the rest: hands off.

KREY: *Basta!*

SCHIPPEL: *(Appalled)* That's it? Ah, so that's it! *(Excited, he pounds his fist on the table.)*

HICKETIER and KREY. Sir!

WOLKE: What's this?

SCHIPPEL *exits.* Meeting's adjourned!

KREY: *(In consternation)* What was that?

WOLKE: The man refuses, game over.

HICKETIER: We're no better off than before.

WOLKE: Net result: we're done for. He laid out his, so to speak, conditions: with great care, I might even say with feminine delicacy. But Hicketier has to lose his temper and break up the party and the deal's dead as a doornail.

HICKETIER: This fellow seems determined to tear down the iron walls between the classes.

KREY: We might have made a few concessions and still maintained the requisite distance.

WOLKE: And his talk was full of please and thank you.

HICKETIER: Through it all I could hear a demand for personal contact, for gross familiarity. *(Beside himself)* Is the fellow allowed to pat me on the back in front of all the world? Have you no sense of shame? If we give this brute a finger, he'll cling to us like a leech. Damn, how poor people stink! Open the window.

WOLKE: And that A, my dear fellow? Hasn't it dawned on you that note sews up the song contest, so to speak, we're the winners in all but name?

KREY: Of course, that's just the point. Naumann couldn't hold a candle to him.

HICKETIER: Even if half my heart were set on it— I can't stomach him. No more than I would rub elbows with the nobility, such familiarity is inconceivable to me, it would horrify me. I like to have my boundaries clearly marked, upper and lower.

We've buried Naumann. Today I think we have to acknowledge an even greater loss: the burial of our dearest, most constant dream.

WOLKE: Is there no way out but Schnippel?

KREY: None, as we well know. It's less than two weeks to the festival and no tenor around but him.

HICKETIER: Once he got to know us this fellow might have the gall to cosy up to our womenfolk. How could the very existence of such a mongrel be made known to a young woman—good God! To Thekla?

WOLKE: And yet your heart is breaking.

HICKETIER: No funeral oration. Two in one day is too much to take. Let's call it fate. Life has no safety nets. *(Exit)*

WOLKE: Thekla! There you have it! Sooner or later he might allow Schippel contact with himself. But Thekla, the defenseless damsel, the, so to speak, untouchable Miss Hicketier!

KREY: So what?

WOLKE: Can you deny that Naumann's death means she's no longer protected from his sort, and that was the deciding factor?

KREY: So what?

WOLKE: I repeat, we're alone; you can speak out.

KREY: Stop your fooling.

WOLKE: You mustn't take masculine delicacy too far.

KREY: God Almighty!

WOLKE: You love Thekla. And if Hicketier knew her to be in your care, at your side…

KREY: What a criminal suggestion. Just because I haven't got your gift of gab I have to put up with this bad joke. It's you, not me, that loves the woman.

WOLKE: No, it's you.

KREY: She's a torment to me, her very presence makes me sick. Her look, her breath are repulsive.

WOLKE: I know what's going on in your heart.

KREY: Sodom and Gomorrah! My life is so nice and cosy and you…

WOLKE: You love her! Ask for her hand! This is the moment of truth!

KREY: You love her! I've known it since day one.

WOLKE: You love her! And even if you blared your denial through Gabriel's horn I know you love her, and I implore you: save this risky situation by yielding to your own blissful happiness.

KREY: (*Hurrying away*) I'll hang myself first!

WOLKE: *(After him)* You hot-tempered savage, you pigheaded egotist. I won't let you.

(Outside a confused noise can be heard. KREY immediately opens the door and steps into the entry way with a deep bow.)

(Enter the PRINCE, age 20, in uniform. KREY and WOLKE follow him into the room.)

PRINCE: Whose house have I invaded? So far as I can tell…

KREY: *(With another bow)* Hicketier's, your serene Highness.

PRINCE: Get a strip of linen, a basin of water. Send a message to the castle for the doctor to attend to me.

(The PRINCE drops into an armchair, opens the torn sleeve of his tunic. Suddenly stares fixedly at WOLKE. KREY has gone out.)

WOLKE: *(Shyly pressed against the wall, with a deep bow.)* Wolke.

PRINCE: How so? —Damned runaway, can't be reined in. I steered him hard against the long wall of this house, grazed it, put on the brakes, in a manner of speaking. And some brave fellow grabbed hold of him. The beast came to a halt.

WOLKE: *(Beaming)* Outstanding!

PRINCE: Crowbait! I'll keep a tight rein on him from now on.

(HICKETIER and KREY enter bowing.)

HICKETIER: What a thing to happen…I am honored, your Highness.

PRINCE: Water, a bandage… A woman would be best.

HICKETIER: My wife is hurrying to get it.

WOLKE: *(With a deep bow)* Wolke!

PRINCE: So I've heard. Is there a point to it? So, Herr Hicketier?

HICKETIER: How can I be of service?

PRINCE: Runaway! Bruise bleeding. Day's off to a bad start. Old woman crossed my path, raindrops pelting down, gray clouds… *(He smiles at* WOLKE.[3]*)* Now I get it— Overcast… *(He sinks down.)*

KREY *jumps up.* Highness! He's fainted.

*(*HICKETIER *and* WOLKE *run around the room to no purpose, then head for the door just as* JENNY *and* THEKLA *enter.* JENNY *brings a basin of water,* THEKLA *cloth for bandages.* THEKLA *kneels before the* PRINCE, *takes his dangling arm, begins to cleanse and bind it, while* JENNY *is busy trying to revive the unconscious man.)*

PRINCE: Rein 'im in. What's this? A heavenly apparition?

*(*THEKLA *completes her work neatly.)*

PRINCE: Kindness itself. Loveliness and grace. Charmante.

(The women leave the room.)

HICKETIER: Highness, she studied nursing.

PRINCE: Charité itself, I tell you. Never knew. Meaning of the word till today. A masterpiece of bandaging. Charmante. Ticked me off. That damned horse! *(He rises, reaches for his cap.)* Sorry, didn't I have a whip? *(To* WOLKE*)* Why do you keep saying Wolke?

KREY: His name, Highness. Proprietor of a printing works.

3   WOLKE *means clouds. Every time the name is mentioned, the* PRINCE *thinks it has to do with the weather.*

PRINCE: Ah—our Wolke! The blue shop-sign in the market place: All kinds of printing performed at high speed.

WOLKE: At low prices.

PRINCE: Delighted. Where did the ladies get to?

HICKETIER: My wife, my sister Thekla.

PRINCE: Thek... My dear Herr Hicketier, we have heard of you. Once it often...

HICKETIER: Highness, when I was a boy his late Highness...

PRINCE: I'll come back to that. So this is Herr Wolke. No subversive pamphlets? Nothing Socialist, anarchist?

WOLKE: Out of the question, Highness.

KREY: Civil assessor Krey.

PRINCE: Bravo! The propertied class, gentlemen, the civil service— hm. The lady who came to my aid? Why withhold an opportunity to thank her?

HICKETIER: Right away. *Exits.*

PRINCE: *(Notices the wreath)* A golden wreath. Some sort of...

KREY: The singing prize won twice by our quartet.

PRINCE: My father's famous vocal group. The local Meistersinger, so to speak.
Calls to mind my oversight: two weeks from now— I know— and the prize song is still to be decided. *(To himself:)* We're wallowing in the deadliest boredom with such an amusing event right under our nose. *(Aloud)* The men's choir, an important institution, dear to the hearts of the people, cannot be held in high enough regard by all of us. It must vigorously repel the onslaught of these times so barren of ideals. The

German Lied, gentlemen! With this in mind we make the extraordinary resolution to dignify the coming festival by our princely presence. *(To himself:)* Good heavens, what am I thinking? *(Aloud:)* You won it twice. I hope most earnestly that the wreath will not pass from you; the victory must certainly be yours this time as well.

(WOLKE and KREY bow.)

(HICKETIER enters with JENNY and THEKLA.)

PRINCE: These gentlemen have heard my opinion regarding the prize song, my dear Hicketier. *(Bows to JENNY and kisses her hand.)* Dear lady! *(Bows to THEKLA)* Charité. May Heaven watch over you! *(Very quietly to her:)* Thekla! *(Exits with a salute)*

(They all stand bowing deeply. THEKLA drops into the armchair in which the PRINCE sat. Since she is turned away, she goes unnoticed by the others on stage.)

WOLKE: My legs are like jelly.

HICKETIER: That's where he stood.

KREY: *(To HICKETIER)* Your roof over the Prince's head.

JENNY: I hope the wound heals quickly.

KREY: And how simply, how informally he behaved.

WOLKE: How affably: our Wolke. His very own Wolke, in a manner of speaking.

HICKETIER: From another, higher realm.

WOLKE: "You must win the song competition, gentlemen." Charmant.

HICKETIER: Did he say that?

KREY: Indeed he did, commanded it without contradiction. With a piercing glance.

WOLKE: Piercing but affable. The German Lied versus anarchy. Charmant. No one but you must win the wreath.

JENNY: *(To* HICKETIER*)* Now come to the table. *(Exit)*

KREY: How is one to carry out such an irresistible command?

HICKETIER: He made it to one of you.

WOLKE: *(To* HICKETIER*)* Let's not be coy: you're the powerhouse in our group. Only you can find the ways and means to coax Schippel, without us losing face somehow.

KREY: For, whatever our personal desires, now it's a matter of the Prince's honor or dishonor.

HICKETIER: But…

WOLKE: The Prince! Ah, Hicketier, even if he hadn't shown up—look me in the eye—you would not have stood back and refused to make our dreams come true.

KREY: You can't go on living till you've persuaded that Schippel.

WOLKE: And you've got the gift of gab.

HICKETIER *after a pause.* Why not! Passions are running high once more. So I'll put honor and conscience to one side and take charge again.

WOLKE *quietly to him.* And I have a suggestion about Thekla too.

HICKETIER *laughs.* Why am I not surprised?

WOLKE: Give me your hands. In view of the importance of the cause, let us swear.

HICKETIER, KREY & WOLKE: *(Far downstage, holding each other's hands, simultaneously:)* We swear!

KREY: What an ordeal! I'm feeling better.

WOLKE: An eventful morning. But a crisis and fight hone a man's appetite. Hicketier's a force of nature, eh?

HICKETIER: I still have to prove it by facing down that monster. And now to the table, gentlemen. *(Exits)*

KREY: We have to talk privately.

WOLKE: What for?

KREY: Fraud, horse-trader!

WOLKE: My motives are above reproach.

(They exit.)

(THEKLA leaps from the chair to the window and throws it open. She leans out. Suddenly she raises her hand and waves a handkerchief.)

END OF ACT ONE

ACT TWO

(The same room)

(THEKLA alone. There is a rap on the window. She rushes over, opens it halfway. An arm is seen, handing in a letter. She takes it, closes the window. Peruses the writing)

THEKLA: At ten tonight he wants to…oh God!

WOLKE: *(Entered just as THEKLA took in the letter)* I'd like to know if your brother is back, if it's not too much to ask.

THEKLA: To cut short any mystery-making on your part—here!

(THEKLA hands WOLKE the letter.)

WOLKE: *(Doesn't take it)* For heaven's sake, Thekla! It's quite all right. It's all in tune with the divine harmony of the universe. A birthday greeting wafting in the window, to which I add my own. Besides, I know all about it. My knowledge of human nature revealed the secret a few days before it became obvious. I threw the lover's infatuation in his face.

THEKLA: You—whose?

WOLKE: I know what your tone of voice implies. So let me make a clean breast of it at once. You're aware that since I was a boy I've not been indifferent to you either. And this heartfelt affection will certainly never lessen in my lifetime. But then I noticed in Krey…

THEKLA: Krey?

WOLKE: Whenever you're around his pretending he's not in the room, that very peculiar je ne sais quoi, how's it go?

THEKLA: You're saying Krey—and then—you as well?

WOLKE: A tragic situation. In all sincerity and conscience I admit Krey is so utterly superior to me in every way that I held back. You may suspect that Krey employed me to say this, but I swear my own heart compels me, his perfect manliness, worth, importance, upright character, honesty, ambition, his iron will, but then too his noble restraint in this particular case, restraint not only in this instance…

THEKLA: I've always found him pleasant enough. But you say restraint. Is he so lacking in imagination?

WOLKE: Krey lacking in imagination? Oh my goodness me, the extravagant notions this man has! His every move expresses the unspoken grandeur of his mental processes. Not restraint, but such a degree of modesty I'm afraid we'll almost have to force him to confess his passion. And so, I would also like you, Thekla…

THEKLA: To encourage him? *(To herself)* Could this nonsense further my plans? *(Aloud)* The things you ask of a young woman…

WOLKE: Friendship compels me. What this renunciation costs me— may be expressed in a word or two, but it is hard for the heart to comply. *(He has taken hold of her hand and kissed it.)*

THEKLA: I shall try to follow your instructions. *(Laughing silently to herself she exits.)*

WOLKE: Right on target. If his foolish nature keeps the truth wrapped up like a mummy, his mouth will have to be pried open.

(JENNY *enters.*)

WOLKE: Isn't he back from Schippel's yet?

JENNY: Last night he never stopped moaning and groaning. He was grappling with a ghost in his sleep.

WOLKE: For a man in pain a dynamic yet cautious struggle is preferable to silently repressing one's feelings, as Krey does.

JENNY: Is the situation making him suffer too?

WOLKE: That and something else. Just now a letter from Krey to Thekla wafted in through the window.

JENNY: A clandestine correspondence. Are you raving!

WOLKE: You know me, Jenny, to be of sound mind. I held the note in my own hand: he loves her.

JENNY: Impossible.

WOLKE: Black on white. And in such a tone of respect, such a sense of honor…

JENNY: Tilmann won't stand for it. He was less than willing to give her to Naumann, who was much closer to him than Krey.

WOLKE: But Krey's brilliant qualities! The vehement force of his passion. I implore you in the name of our friendship…

JENNY: First let's settle this Schippel business. What about Thekla herself?

WOLKE: She didn't exactly say so, but I'd be a poor judge of character if I didn't sense the lovebird fluttering in her charming self.

JENNY: Then, of course, I promise to assist you. She mentioned a man crouching by the fence last night, staring up at her.

WOLKE: That must have been Krey! Q.E.D.

HICKETIER: *(Enters)* Victory! I turn into Windisch Street, there stands Schippel who tips his hat as casual as you please. So I manage to sort things out in a couple of words and now a meeting's arranged. He's on his way.

JENNY: Thank goodness!

HICKETIER: I would have brought him with me, because now every second matters.

WOLKE: The audition's still to be held today.

HICKETIER: First he had to leave a message, but he's right behind me. As it happens, our situation has been weighing on his mind, he'd read the Prince's decree concerning the festival in yesterday's paper and learned it by heart. *(To* JENNY*)* You open the door; no one must see him come here as a regular visitor. *(She exits.)*

WOLKE: And what I was saying about Thekla still goes.

HICKETIER: I appreciate your concern and guess your intentions; but put it aside until this cliff-hanger of a dilemma is settled. Incidentally, Krey was making similar hints about you.

WOLKE: Impossible!

HICKETIER: So don't confuse me. To sort this out I have to keep a clear head.

WOLKE: And let us know the result of your confab with Schippel right away. We're dying to know.

HICKETIER: At once. Have you seen the birthday girl?

WOLKE: Through a cloud of sorrow over what has been lost the first ray of hope now seems to dawn.

HICKETIER: How poetic.

*(*WOLKE *gives* HICKETIER *his hand, exits.)*

HICKETIER: He loves Thekla. *(Takes from his desk a golden bracelet, and holds it up to the light, next to the wreath)* A perfect replica of the original. Even if I were to lose the wreath, I should never lose the replacement I made for Thekla. What will she say to my ingenuity?

(THEKLA *enters.*)

HICKETIER: I was just about to call you. Come in.

THEKLA: What's that?

HICKETIER: Crafted by my own hands. Guess who it's for?

THEKLA: For me, as usual?

(THEKLA *sits on* HICKETIER's *lap.*)

HICKETIER: Since the ties that bound the child Thekla to me will loosen as time passes—do you grasp the meaning of my gift?

THEKLA: *(Her arms around his neck.)* I'm as fond of you as ever.

HICKETIER: And that love of brother and sister, as the Hicketier spirit fades with every passing day, shall be symbolized by this golden bracelet. When you are alone, it will remind you…

THEKLA: That's depressing and pointless. Even without it I won't forget my background and my childhood.

HICKETIER: The women in our family have rarely flourished. Will power in the men seems in them to turn to foolish fancies. Even after you marry, the closer you cling to me, the more intimately you will relate to me, the more your nature and your needs will be satisfied.

THEKLA: A great part of me never leaves you, however much and however often I may be attracted to someone else.

HICKETIER: And you feel it will remain so?

THEKLA: Not such serious talk on my birthday.

HICKETIER: Let me have my way. *(He takes her arm.)* When other people are around, slip it under your clothes. *(Slips the bracelet under her sleeve)* Your family home must always be your refuge. Here your most secret thoughts can run free. May a handshake seal your promise forever! *(Handshake)* And now listen, you rascal; you've been the widowed fiancée for barely two seconds and already someone else is after you.

THEKLA: I know…

HICKETIER: With your looks it's only natural that every man wants you. Not to mention an honorable name and a sack of gold into the bargain. What are your admirer's prospects?

THEKLA: *(Extremely embarrassed)* For heaven's sake! *(And runs away.)*

HICKETIER: Well, well! A wonderful girl. *(Exits in the opposite direction)*

*(*JENNY *shows in* SCHIPPEL *and exits left.)*

SCHIPPEL: *(Stands in the center of the room, looks in all directions)* It's hard to believe. Comforts I've been starved of for the last thirty years. No more drifting in the wind, overnight I've become a name to reckon with, someone to be proud of. I'll bet fat Hicketier drifted off to sleep last night with the thought: Schippel's a friend of mine! *(He slinks around the room.)* Plush furniture! Your owners are in business with me. I'm allowed to loll around on you. *(Sprawls in an armchair)* Or thumb through a photo album at my leisure. *(He begins to leaf through a photo album.)* Anybody comes in, I'll stand up, say casually: How'do; I belong here, I was invited, practically dragged in. Decent people for the most part, well connected, honorable, respectable. Gold brooches and watch-chains. Hefty signet rings. Good afternoon, sir, delighted to make your acquaintance: I'm a friend of the family, can come and go as I please. Why, Herr Schippel! Just a belch, my dear pastor. After a good meal it's permitted among friends.

HICKETIER: *(Enters)* To explain my behavior yesterday—

SCHIPPEL: Never mind. What's done is done. Today's another day.

HICKETIER: Just as well. We were worried that despite your splendid vocal abilities, what with your background you might not grasp the historical significance of the prize song...

SCHIPPEL: What you say hurts my feelings.

HICKETIER: I won't mince words.

SCHIPPEL: Don't hold back if we're to arrive as a real understanding. But we may be in luck and the song will simply be about rambling around or plain old love of woods and fields, which I'm capable of interpreting as a result of my—how did you put it?

HICKETIER: Where did you learn breath control, phrasing?

SCHIPPEL: From my flute. The way the stops snap open and shut, I imitate with my throat.

HICKETIER: You rehearse in front of a mirror?

SCHIPPEL: Know my vocal chords inside-out. The uvula works like a glockenspiel.

HICKETIER: So shall we give it a try?

SCHIPPEL: Put myself entirely at the disposal of the cause.

HICKETIER: Bravo. Just one more word about how to behave in public.

SCHIPPEL: I get the picture. Put on the brakes. Easy does it!

HICKETIER: In me you see someone rooted in tradition. My feet on the ground. I like things to develop gradually.

SCHIPPEL: Got it. Not like me, shot up in a flash from nowhere to the top, my head wobbling, as the saying goes, on a slender stalk. Keep a lid on. Got it. Mustn't give in when I get the urge…

HICKETIER: Take it easy.

SCHIPPEL: To snatch and grab…

(SCHIPPEL *holds out his arms to* HICKETIER.)

HICKETIER: What's come over you?

SCHIPPEL: *(Hypnotically)* Or pat you on the stomach, don't flinch! *(He claps him on the stomach.)* Morning, Hicketier old man.

HICKETIER: *(Hypnotized)* How dare you—who do you think…

SCHIPPEL: *(Pulling himself together)* Under no circumstances act that vulgar, got it. Always three steps to the rear.

HICKETIER: *(Beside himself)* Behave, manners! Or else—!

SCHIPPEL: Anyway. I'll sing. Warble like an angel. All set. No one'll beat us… When?

HICKETIER: Tonight at eight here.

SCHIPPEL: All right. Done.

HICKETIER: And always on condition you behave in future according to my express wishes, I'll keep yesterday's promise and put coin in your pocket. Let me get twenty marks from the cash-drawer. *(Exits)*

SCHIPPEL: A throwback to the past, the dear old relic. Yesterday I was still a rabbit, cowering in the cabbage-patch. But now such terrific energy surges inside me my toes are turning into knives, my teeth into sabers.

Dealing with me will bruise you black and blue, and I'm afraid I'm going to make a shambles of your neat and tidy parlor.

(THEKLA *crosses from right to left and, not noticing* SCHIPPEL *who bows to her, goes into her room.*)

SCHIPPEL: (*Imitating her stiff-backed stride follows the same path and stops center stage*) Wafting by on clean undies. Marking the gulf between her and me. What's that you smell of, my pouter pigeon? (*He walks the rest of* THEKLA's *path, sniffing.*) Fresh as a daisy!

HICKETIER: (*Returns*) Who went out?

(HICKETIER *hands* SCHIPPEL *a gold piece.*)

SCHIPPEL: (*Takes it, laughing*) If you only knew…

HICKETIER Was it…?

SCHIPPEL: A pretty little wagtail. If you'd been here a moment sooner, you would have had to make a formal introduction.

HICKETIER: There will never be any suggestion of that. When it comes to family matters, my private life is out of bounds.

SCHIPPEL: Stands to reason. Except…

HICKETIER: What?

SCHIPPEL: Singing tonight at eight here.

HICKETIER: Except? Say what's on your mind.

SCHIPPEL: Mum's the word. Something crazy. Whenever I'm in your parlor I feel packed with dynamite. (*He roars with laughter.*) Packed with dynamite's a good one, right? But I know how it goes: quick exit, explode outside. See you tonight. (*Exit*)

HICKETIER: (*Shudders*) Except? If you only knew? What?— Thekla came through here— I've got goose-bumps all over. (*He calls into the room up left.*) Jenny!

(JENNY *enters.*)

HICKETIER: Too many men will be traipsing through the house between now and the song contest. The girl will go to her aunt in Naumburg today.

JENNY: Krey slipped a letter to her through the window today.

HICKETIER: Krey? Pack her bags at once, this minute. Send her here.

(JENNY *exits.*)

HICKETIER: Krey too? Even the dullest goats are hankering after her. Wolke *and* Krey? A letter through the window? And she didn't say a word when we were so close earlier.

(THEKLA *enters from her room.*)

HICKETIER: Give me Krey's letter.

(THEKLA *keeps silent.*)

HICKETIER: Hand over the letter.

THEKLA: It isn't from him, Tilmann.

HICKETIER: Then it's from Wolke. Give it to me. (*Reproachfully*) Why behind my back?

THEKLA: (*Looks at* HICKETIER *calmly.*) It isn't from Wolke.

HICKETIER: Not from Wolke— or Krey— good God! (*Drops on to a chair, jumps up again and says:*) No no no! Say it isn't so!

THEKLA: What for?

HICKETIER: Girl— I'm losing my mind. Out with it— it was all my fault. So worried about the wreath I neglected you. Who's it from? Thekla!

(HICKETIER *and* THEKLA *stand close together, staring deep into one another's eyes.*)

HICKETIER: *(Whispers)* Schippel?

THEKLA: You *are* losing your mind! *(And is about to go.)*

HICKETIER: *(Grabs her, pulls her to him and says:)* Then who?

THEKLA: *(Standing up to him)* My business! *(Runs out, slamming the door.)*

HICKETIER: A wolf in the flock! She's got to go away. But whoever he is, I'll catch him!

END OF ACT TWO

ACT THREE

(The courtyard garden behind HICKETIER's *house, bordered on the right by a fence. Evening)*

PRINCE: *(In a black cloak appears right. Beneath her window, hugging the house wall.)* Thekla!

THEKLA: There he is!

PRINCE: Keep to the edge of the woods, step by step. The peace of mind of my Gentleman of the Bedchamber must not be ruffled. The hardest part was having to slip past five, six houses with their lights on. My subjects still not asleep. I'll have to make a law against it.

THEKLA: We have a parliament, noble sir.

PRINCE: So young women are into politics?

THEKLA: Nowadays they receive a comprehensive education. They know the natural sciences and can read a railroad time-table. But princes who sneak up to windows at night exist only in fairy tales, or so they're told.

PRINCE: If anyone stops me and asks, I'm Harun al-Rashid, gathering information about his people. Would they believe me capable of it?

THEKLA: People picture you as a melancholic, which goes with night and a black cloak.

PRINCE: Does Thekla think I'm gloomy?

THEKLA: Any such assumption is contradicted by the monocle the Prince wears even at night. But he can't see without it, he might reply. A truly gloomy man gazes only into the abyss of his own heart.

PRINCE: It's becoming, women tell me.

THEKLA: The princes I know are in folk songs, with a shining sword by their side. And when they appear beneath a young girl's window, they also clasp a dagger. A girl's self-respect demands a dagger.

PRINCE: Then I'm more like Eberhard of Württemburg, who dare lay his head, unarmed, in any subject's lap. Can Thekla guess my fondest wish at this moment?

THEKLA: To be Eberhard of Württemburg?

PRINCE: No one else.

THEKLA: Because you assumed great responsibility when still but a boy, the people love you.

PRINCE: Bravo. Are you the people, Thekla?

THEKLA: I am.

PRINCE: A subject?

THEKLA: A subject.

PRINCE: Get down here at once! Now I'm acting like a character in Shakespeare. Have fallen for you and bark an order at you.

THEKLA: Ah, Shakespeare is old hat. We're three centuries beyond him.

PRINCE: Then how do modern poets treat this sort of thing?

THEKLA: If you want to be convincing, parliament must play a part, because you are a constitutional monarch.

PRINCE: Suppose I summon parliament?

THEKLA: What about the Social Democrats?

PRINCE: There's only one. He'll be outvoted. All the rest do whatever I want.

THEKLA: Only the assembled law-makers will first have to sweep my brother and his cronies out of the house, for they stand in my way.

PRINCE: Why aren't they in bed?

THEKLA: Most important business. The quartet is newly reconstituted. In two weeks the Prince's laurel wreath will be in play. A tenor is replacing the one who just died.

PRINCE: This singing business will allow me to maintain an official connection with your family over the next few weeks. I shall grant your brother an audience tomorrow morning. Hush!

(Moving shadows have been visible behind a lighted picture window on the ground floor. Now SCHIPPEL*'s silhouette can be discerned in the window.* SCHIPPEL*'s voice sings:)*
SCHIPPEL:
Hark, the lark sings in the grove.
Listen, listen, lady love,
Listen, listen, lady love.
Ope thy casement on the sly,
Hearken, hearken, be not shy,
Hearken, hearken, be not shy.[4]

(In the room, sound of applause)

PRINCE: Splendidly sung. Why hasn't such a voice brought fame to our court theatre?

THEKLA: The singer is a bastard.

---

4   "Horch, die Lerche singt im Hain" from Nicolai's *Die Lustige Weiber von Windsor (The Merry Wives of Windsor)*.

PRINCE: Shakespeare again! Bastards are his specialty.
Princes and bastards. You no longer dare deny
this is an historic occasion. Even my monocle has
disappeared..

THEKLA: The telegraph poles over there still spoil the
mood.

PRINCE: But what can they do against a bastard, a
prince and—amazing! Here's a dagger as well. Not
much more than a hunting knife, but with a little
effort...

THEKLA: Which I have.

PRINCE: We need a ladder.

THEKLA: Over there in the shed. Wait! No one's ever
heard of Harun al-Rashid climbing a ladder.

PRINCE: It's a variant.

THEKLA: And the maiden's honor?

PRINCE: Is concealed beneath the sultan's cloak.

THEKLA: A ladder and a living room—that's not very
romantic.

PRINCE: A living room and a ladder—just as middle-
class as I had imagined.

(HICKETIER *has stepped into the window frame, pulled aside
the curtain, looks out into the night. In the background*
SCHIPPEL, KREY *and* WOLKE *can be seen at the piano.*)

THEKLA: Don't be silly. I don't dare. I had the most
distressing scene with my brother. The letter was
discovered. Of course, to calm him down, I lied to my
sister-in-law that it was the Prince's thanks for the help
we'd given him yesterday. Even so, I've got to go away
first thing tomorrow. He's scared.

PRINCE: Of whom?

THEKLA: Who do you think?

PRINCE: Are you scared?

(HICKETIER *has disappeared from the window.*)

THEKLA: I love Tilmann. Upsetting him is the hardest thing for me.

PRINCE: So I'm intruding on your peace and quiet. Luring an angel to tell lies.

THEKLA: Since yesterday every breath I take is a sin. But a Prince! A young and melancholy hero. A prince appears so often in the folk songs I've sung with my brother that I was his, long before he actually showed up.

PRINCE: Is he what you expected?

THEKLA: Totally.

PRINCE: That's a confession, Thekla.

THEKLA: It was supposed to be. Would I be speaking out of a window at night otherwise?

PRINCE: Trust me?

THEKLA: Absolutely.

PRINCE: Listen: tomorrow I'll meet you at the hunting lodge next to the bridle path.

THEKLA: I have to go away. There's no point.

PRINCE: You mustn't. Not tomorrow. Not before we meet again. Between six and seven in the morning no one in the house will miss you. I'll ride down the bridle path in a green coat, a hat with a green brush, and a hunting knife at my side—is that romantic enough? If you want, I'll put on a medal; the little gold wreath I got from the Kaiser, my dear cousin and fellow-prince.

THEKLA: And how am I to dress?

PRINCE: I picture you in calico. No frills. Come to me as a member of your class. You are divinely perfect, just the way you are.

THEKLA: *(Hums)*
Her slender neck white, her dark eyes bright,
With golden tresses all bedight.
Her precious body pale as ermine…[5]

PRINCE: When I'm with you I really feel a part of such
music, and the business with your brother, the singing
for the wreath, bourgeois ambition, go straight to
my heart. Our forests, our little towns are where the
elemental music of such Lieder abides and it enchants
us with its verve.

THEKLA: They were born here among us and stay with
us all our lives long. This realm of ours has the loveliest
songs. They're in all the traditional songsters.

PRINCE: And so the prince of this land is duty-bound to
cherish them truly.

THEKLA: I'll teach you from the ground up.

PRINCE: And tomorrow we'll choose the very best for
the song competition.

(The QUARTET in the room sings. We can see HICKETIER
conducting with a baton, the other three in the middle.)

QUARTET:
What pleasure on earth with the hunter's compares?
Whose cup of life sparkles so rich and so fair?
To lie in the greenwood and hear the horns sound,
To follow the stag through each thicket and pond,

5   Lines from the folksong "Meiner Frauen roter
Mund" (*"My wife's red mouth"*) in *Der Knaben
Wunderhorn (The Lad's Magic Horn, 1805-08),* a famous
collection of folk poems and songs collected by Achim
von Arnim and Clemens Brentano.

Is joy for a prince, is a real man's desire,
It strengthens your limbs and your appetite fires—[6]

(The PRINCE *reaches out his hands;* THEKLA *offers hers.)*

PRINCE: Joy for a prince! A real man's desire!

QUARTET:
When woodland and rocks resound all the day long,
A brimming cup sings a freer and happier song.

THEKLA: The ladder, quick bring the ladder!

(The PRINCE *brings out the ladder.)*

QUARTET:
Yohohoho, tralala…

THEKLA: Look away! I'm coming down.

*(*THEKLA *does so quickly. The* PRINCE *catches and embraces her.)*

QUARTET:
Tralala tralala tralalala *(Etc)*

THEKLA: Put away the ladder!

(The PRINCE *moves it to one side.)*

THEKLA: Where can we go? Behind the cart. If anyone comes, it will hide us.

PRINCE: *(Embraces* THEKLA*)* You are the loved one, just as you are. Dress, apron—the perfect picture.

THEKLA: And the right size too.

PRINCE: The right eyes…

THEKLA: The right hair…

PRINCE: The right mouth… *(He kisses her.)* Say something.

6   The huntsmen's chorus,"Was gleicht wohl auf Erden dem Jägervergnügen," from *Der Freischütz (The Enchanted Sharpshooter)* by Weber.

THEKLA: You're too aristocratic, proud.

PRINCE: Not proud. *(He moves as if to kneel down beside her.)*

THEKLA: Stooping to conquer… *(And bows down too)*

PRINCE: Oh maiden…

THEKLA: *(Kisses him)* Sweetheart.

PRINCE: My name!

THEKLA: Henry the Fourth.

PRINCE: Forget the number— I hope I'm the first.

THEKLA: The one and only.

(The PRINCE and THEKLA stand beside the cart and then disappear behind it into the open shed.)

(HICKETIER, SCHIPPEL, KREY and WOLKE walk out the door.)

WOLKE: No beating around the bush: he's phenomenal. Krey? What's your opinion?

KREY: Not bad.

WOLKE: Cantilena, timbre— You're shaken to your core, Hicketier.

HICKETIER: I didn't expect so much. There can be no doubt as to the outcome of the song contest. It's as good as won.

WOLKE: Yet how his voice fits in with ours. Such harmony was never the case with Naumann. *(To SCHIPPEL)* You know the fairy tale? You can say with the Emperor of China's nightingale: I've seen tears in your eyes.

SCHIPPEL: True enough. There was one in yours. *(He takes him by the coat button.)*

WOLKE: It can't be denied; your E sent shivers down my spine.

HICKETIER: The male voice, especially in the upper registers, is one of God's greatest miracles. Little else goes so straight to my heart.

WOLKE: Tenderer than a maiden's touch. *(To* KREY*)* Don't be ashamed of your emotions.

KREY: Don't exaggerate.

HICKETIER: Let's retire while the impression is still warm. Good night. *(He turns to go back into the house.)*

KREY: Good night.

*(*KREY *goes with* WOLKE *towards the gate in the fence.)*

SCHIPPEL: *(Follows them, turns to* HICKETIER*)* Hey there!

HICKETIER: Sorry?

SCHIPPEL: *(Hesitant)* Hm…

WOLKE: What's up?

SCHIPPEL: Nothing actually.

WOLKE: Come along then.

*(*WOLKE *pulls* SCHIPPEL *towards the fence.)* With a tenor like this, Krey, it'd be worth having your composition performed.

KREY: *(To* SCHIPPEL*)* He's lying through his teeth, I never composed a note.

WOLKE: *(To* SCHIPPEL*)* He'll never admit to his merits. But even so you must have noticed them by now. What did you want with Hicketier?

SCHIPPEL: *(With a glance at* HICKETIER*)* Something that mattered at the time, but I clean forgot it. Ha ha…

*(*SCHIPPEL, KREY, WOLKE *exit.)*

HICKETIER: *(Stands in the middle of the yard and stares up at* THEKLA's *window)* No good-night, doesn't even let me see her. That's how it will be for days and weeks. I was too headstrong over that letter, too rash. The

Prince's thanks for yesterday's help. She must have heard us singing; she must be moved, in a state of flux. In her little head, in her bosom love and rebellion are contending. Child, child, are you asleep already? But in a flash I was worried about you, I couldn't breathe. Don't know what it means. If I force my way into the chaos in her soul, I'll spoil everything. If only I could be near her to hear. *(He hums:)*
To hear, to hear her heart's desire...
Such sweet melody from that proletarian breast! Not cracked or wobbly the way the rabble sings, but at peace with the world and everything in it.
May all good spirits bless you! Your brother, his heart still racked with second thoughts, only wanted—understand me in your dreams. Good night. *(He kisses his hand to the window and goes into the house.)*

PRINCE: *(Visible next to the cart)* Nobody here. Will my lady deign to emerge from the shadows of our hovel and bestow her presence on these brightly lighted premises?

THEKLA: *(Voice)* I shun premises, light and atmosphere. May this night never end!

(The PRINCE disappears again.)

SCHIPPEL: *(Surfaces by the fence)* Look at that house sprawling broad in the beam over the earth! They overcharge us for every inch of ground; here an empty cart stands idly by on a whole half an acre. *(With raised fist:)* I hate you! The way you stuff your gullet with handfuls of sweets, you lazy bourgeois swine, void your guts and go on gorging until, crammed with nutritious sap, you pass on to your children that hard and shiny surface, the result of over-fed nerves, that pollutes the world. Meanwhile, more often than not, we have to sweat and strain to spawn a single litter. No chance of a posterity whose blood might pass

on one valuable asset, the memory of our ferocious
indignation, and so might be able to mow you down!
(He goes into the yard.) My limbs are shivering in these
rags. That bourgeois girl's skirt was stretched to
bursting over her hips. *(Once again he copies* THEKLA's
walk. Then he strokes the house wall.) No wind can blow
through here, the walls two feet thick. On the inside
of the wall bulge portraits of father and grandfather.
Born 1838, died '86. I don't have the one, the other's a
blank... You slithered out of my grasp before, old man.
I had fantastic plans for you, tried to break the bank,
my palm was itching. Now I'm itching to get at you
again, all the way, so my breath will blow in your face.
I'm longing for you down here, you obese, narrow-
minded snob. Spew a self-righteous bass belch from
your potbelly: I'm in love with you, your whole life-
style, your class. My little heart is pounding, my pulse
racing. *(Notices the ladder)* A ladder! I'll risk it. You have
sex-appeal for the dispossessed, my lord and master,
far stronger than any woman's. *(He leans the ladder
against* THEKLA's *window, climbs up and looks in.)* A
nightie thrown over a chair. The harem! Wrong room.
*(Clambers down in a jiffy, put the ladder up again, climbs up
and looks in another window.)* There he is! All's right with
the world!
Hangs his coat on a hanger, smooths it down pat. Of
course order must prevail throughout the universe.
The suspenders on six firm buttons, make a note,
Schippel. And gray socks with garters.

HICKETIER: *(Throws open the window from inside)* Are you
insane?

SCHIPPEL: Drunk with singing. Still deeply moved from
before. Don't look so shocked, citizen, at a tiny degree
of frenzy.

HICKETIER: You're destroying the good impression you
made. Go home.

SCHIPPEL: What a funny fellow you are. Never understands my intentions. I wanted, ha ha ha, wanted to get a better sense of my good luck.

HICKETIER: Someone would think you've lost all sense. The middle of the night. Next to this window— my sister is sleeping— If she heard you— March! *(Slams the window shut)*

SCHIPPEL: *(Climbs down the ladder)* Military orders. His sister's sleeping— *(He stands in the middle of the yard again.)* Pleasingly plump and in white undies. Son of a bitch, scum! You're trying to put one over on me! *(Storms up the ladder and pounds with his fist on* HICKETIER's *windowpane.)* Snap to it! Up and out of your sound slumbers! The girl next door—she's the one—I want…

(The PRINCE, *and* THEKLA *behind him, unseen by the others, cautiously move to hide beside the cart.)*

HICKETIER: *(His face briefly visible behind the windowpane, appears, storming out the front door on to the stage, dashes to the foot of the ladder and hisses up to* SCHIPPEL.*)* What did you say, you scoundrel?

SCHIPPEL: *(Turns round on the ladder to him)* Your sister! Or else wild horses won't pull a sound out of my gullet!

*(*HICKETIER *darts to the cart, grabs the horsewhip from the coachman's box.)*

(The PRINCE *and* THEKLA *are close to* HICKETIER, *crouching behind the cart.)*

HICKETIER: *(Catches sight of them, shouts out.)* Ah! *(Pulls himself together and stumbles towards* SCHIPPEL.*)* Was the cur barking? Stinking prole!

*(*SCHIPPEL *jumps off the ladder, snatches the whip away from* HICKETIER, *presses him close against the wall and stands face to face with him.)*

SCHIPPEL: *(Frantic:)* Yes, prole, and proud to stink. I'll marry your sister, that stuck-up bitch. I'll plant my red flag over the whole lot of you! Drop dead, old man, hang down your head. To be continued!

(SCHIPPEL storms out the gate in the fence. HICKETIER stands paralyzed.)

(The PRINCE leads THEKLA with a regal gesture into the house. Stops in front of HICKETIER.)

PRINCE: Your sister Thekla—is now too upset— naturally, tomorrow… *(Quickly turns to go)*

END OF ACT THREE

ACT FOUR

(Same setting. Early morning)

*(*HICKETIER *sits in an arbor, asleep.)*

JENNY: *(Appears in the doorway)* I haven't got the heart to wake him.

*(*WOLKE *comes to* JENNY *from the fence.)*

JENNY: *(Points out* HICKETIER *to him)* Ssh!

WOLKE: Goodness!

JENNY: He sat there all night long. When I got up this morning, I didn't find him in his bed.

WOLKE: Worries. Schippel!

JENNY: He puts a brave face on bad business, but in his mind he's going through hell.

WOLKE: These few days before the festival he's got to keep it together. The Wolkes are not to be trifled with either. Did you talk to him about our plan?

JENNY: Which one?

WOLKE: Krey. I'd like to celebrate an engagement and winning the song contest at the same time.

JENNY: You're barking up the wrong tree. Krey reacted with downright rudeness to a subtle hint about his devious night-time maneuver…

WOLKE: That figures! He's a lynx, a fox, a cuckoo. My dear, in love there are psychoses you can't imagine. For instance there's the fanatic who dreams his beloved is in the direst danger, victim of the vilest intrigues, so he imagines he has the courage to rescue her.

JENNY: How nasty!

(HICKETIER, *in his sleep, snores.*)

WOLKE: Bravo! Gradually—and this is what's diabolical about it—he moves so far away from the innocuous reality of his dearly beloved that he no longer cares for her in her normal state. Result: catastrophe. Mother weeps, father wails amidst the ruins. Root cause: the fanatic. Now without wanting to imply it's that way with Krey, he has within him what is called an abnormality, which in this case means his intellectual superiority—

JENNY: You think him so clever!

WOLKE: A universal genius, Jenny! Hear what he has to say about the Jews. Ah, what a brain! Or take technology, physics, algebra and pay close attention to his eyeballs. Those lively pupils, as they flicker and squint, are a clue to the mysterious process.

JENNY: Meaning?

WOLKE: He has elevated Thekla in his mind to be a paragon of perfection. A Platonic ideal. And now he doesn't think himself worthy.

JENNY: And to some degree he's right. She is a Hicketier and a wonderful girl as well.

WOLKE: Peerless and delectable. Granted. Now here's my strategy: I never stopped talking about her, gave him her picture, some writing of hers, filled his world with her spirit, her scent, I—if I may say so—plagued him to death with her. Finally, when the colossus was weak in the knees, last night I let it out that in her crazed desire she had carved his initials in the big elm in the yard.

JENNY: Wolke!

WOLKE: I did it myself this morning between five and six o'clock. Take a look. *(He points to the spot.)*

JENY. But!

WOLKE: I saw Hicketier. He was snoring hard and fast. It instantly gave me some idea of what's he like at the table. And it's a good bet that Krey, before he goes to the office, will show up at any minute to check on it.

JENNY: There he is!

(WOLKE pulls JENNY behind the cart:)

WOLKE: Get back!

KREY: *(Comes in, look cautiously around and runs to the elm.)* True enough! *(He leans against the trunk and wipes the sweat from his brow, groaning.)* How revolting! I'm done for. *(Exits)*

(WOLKE steps out with JENNY:)

WOLKE: Tears? No doubt about it. Yes, dearest friend— I have engineered your happiness. *(Follows him out in an emotional state.)*

JENNY: *(Goes into the arbor and stands facing HICKETIER)* Dear heart.

HICKETIER: *(In his sleep)* Heh?

JENNY: It's past eight.

HICKETIER: *(Abruptly waking)* Thekla?

JENNY: You slept all night here?

HICKETIER: Not a wink.

JENNY: Stop worrying at last. Once you've won the prize, you can wash your hands of Schippel.

HICKETIER: It was an awful dream. Tell me your most secret thoughts.

JENNY: I have none. I'll bring your coffee.

HICKETIER: And Thekla?

JENNY: Should be married.

HICKETIER: God only knows!

JENNY: She's of age. Only with her notions she'll want something special.

HICKETIER: Not a word to anyone, not even to her: Schippel!

JENNY: Tilmann!

HICKETIER: We've buried our heads in the sand. And in the meantime things have gone too far. If I refuse, a catastrophe is guaranteed.

JENNY: Thekla Hicketier—a Schippel! Not on your life…

HICKETIER: No, I have a plan: we'll invent a family tree for the fellow. That disgraced officer, the bachelor who might have been responsible for Schippel's birth, he shall adopt him. His poverty will make him pliable. I'll stake body and soul on it. No questions! You know what's what. Not another word until the bargain's sealed.

JENNY: I was blaming myself— but she was so secretive.

HICKETIER: That she was.

JENNY: Maybe the Prince could do something for Schippel…

HICKETIER: (*Leaps up*) No crumbs from the high and mighty! No whimpering and whining, charity and ultimate embarrassment. With a strong right arm we'll do it all ourselves!

JENNY: God willing. (*Exits*)

(THEKLA *opens her shutters from within. Not fully dressed, she opens her arms wide to the sun beams. The*

golden bracelet can be seen on her upper arm. HICKETIER
walks from the arbor to center stage in silence, facing her.
She removes the bracelet from her arm and tosses it to her
brother.)

HICKETIER: *(Catches it and throws it back. Urgently)*
There's no reason to make such gestures. At this critical
moment no romanticism please. A piece of news
requires an answer: yesterday Herr Schippel asked for
your hand.

(A muffled cry from THEKLA.*)*

HICKETIER: The doubts I once entertained cannot
withstand more practical considerations.

THEKLA: *(Frantically)* Brother…

HICKETIER: Any ifs or buts disappeared last night.
Today, tomorrow, all your life long.

THEKLA: My fate!

HICKETIER: Is to be a middle-class young woman!

THEKLA: I—oh—my heart— *(Buries her face in her hands)*

HICKETIER: *(Suddenly exploding)* No more dreams..
See things in the light of day. Pride, pride, you're
a Hicketier. Consider the hard facts before you get
ridiculously carried away by foolish fancies.

THEKLA: I'm coming down!

(THEKLA bolts from the window, is downstairs at once and
flies into HICKETIER's *arms.)*

THEKLA: Whatever you want. You have my best
interests at heart, I feel it.

HICKETIER: In an hour you'll be far, far away at your
aunt's, stay there until I call you back to honor, peace
and security. Wallow in your sorrow, indulge it to
your heart's content, make a spectacle of yourself
by overdoing it, and don't stop too soon. Keep it

to yourself, though. People like to see their fellow-creatures maintain a stiff upper lip.

(HICKETIER, *his arm around* THEKLA's *shoulders, walks a few paces with her.*)

HICKETIER: When you're a wife, mother or grandmother and you live today over in your mind, your heart must be filled with a sublime awareness of the supreme sacrifice you've made. And later, when I come to call, the self-same smile that plays around your lips behind your tears will remind us who we are, who our ancestors were and what we are capable of. God bless you, child.

(THEKLA *points in the distance, where* SCHIPPEL *appears.*)

SCHIPPEL: *(Calls out)* Good morning all!

THEKLA: Good morning, Herr Schippel. *(Exits)*

HICKETIER: You come as if on cue.

SCHIPPEL: Cued by an inner anxiety. Ever since last night I've been hanging around your house.

HICKETIER: Like a hawk circling its prey.

SCHIPPEL: I crept up that hill and down to the brook and the light from that room *(He points to* THEKLA's *room.)* shone in my eyes the whole time, it never went out. Imagine how I felt!

HICKETIER: How?

SCHIPPEL: Didn't you just say it?

HICKETIER: A hawk!

SCHIPPEL: When I was a kid I'd go up to the other kids in the street. A girl spat in my face: Thekla Hicketier.

HICKETIER: Ah!

SCHIPPEL: The hate that's been welling up in me for twenty years exploded last night uncontrollably, engulfed me in flames. This morning as the brook noisily gurgled, I drowned it out it with sounds I'd never heard me make before. I'll save them for the song competition, because they're the only assurance I'll get the girl. Still, I'd be missing half the pleasure of my satisfied revenge, if I didn't let you know the dreams I dreamed, the moves I made in my imagination, the way I laid hands on her body.

HICKETIER: Quite the fiancé. Now that the girl consents she is yours.

SCHIPPEL: I knew it, when I came upon the two of you.

HICKETIER: And the frankness you've shown today…

SCHIPPEL: Which we share. You will always be ashamed to have me around.

HICKETIER: You catch on quick.

SCHIPPEL: No worries. My view of the world is realistic, down-to-earth. But knowing I've got you in my clutches for the next few days, due to your vanity about the prize, I can manipulate you as I please—

HICKETIER: Playing God.

SCHIPPEL: It's about time.

HICKETIER: Your sails billowing with a favorable wind, so to speak.

SCHIPPEL: I've got spunk and imagination.

HICKETIER: Which you'll try out on Thekla.

SCHIPPEL: Your sister, brother-in-law.

HICKETIER: I'm supposed to be shaking in my shoes?

SCHIPPEL: All signs point to it.

HICKETIER: You're coming too close to me again. To pat my belly. Ha ha ha.

SCHIPPEL: Mentally, my little pal. Doing it's no longer necessary.

HICKETIER: You're straining your pulp fiction fantasies about Thekla too hard. Just because she spat at you...

SCHIPPEL: And then the time will come when she and I stand face to face under my roof, a married couple...

HICKETIER: *(With a loud laugh)* What then?

SCHIPPEL: I threaten her to make her pay, the words clenched in my teeth...

HICKETIER: What then?

SCHIPPEL: I begin...

HICKETIER: Bursting with pride, the puffed-up husband of a Hicketier.

SCHIPPEL: Who had to be spoken to ever so softly. I, a nobody special, born accidentally, grown up in the gutter, now want the middle-class virgin, want to grab hold of her—

(SCHIPPEL grabs HICKETIER.)

HICKETIER: What then?

SCHIPPEL: You old money-bags, is your heart breaking?

HICKETIER: *(With a roar of laughter)* It's laughing at you, the rag-picker who thinks he's come across a flawless gem. Higher laws take you down a peg: what we deign to bestow on you has lost its luster...

(SCHIPPEL draws back.)

HICKETIER: Lost its bloom to a better, a thousand times better man than you.

SCHIPPEL: Thekla...?

HICKETIER: We palm off on you.

(Long pause, in which SCHIPPEL stands turned away)

HICKETIER: *(Business-like)* I owe the newest member of the family an explanation. The size of the dowry we'll talk over in my office as well. *(With a gesture towards the house)* If you will. And I've come up with a way to rectify the serious irregularity of your obscure birth. It concerns the unmarried officer responsible for that blunder.

SCHIPPEL: *(Turns to him)* I take your meaning.

HICKETIER: Bravo.

SCHIPPEL: No need to know more...

HICKETIER: Bravo.

SCHIPPEL: I don't believe the concept of manly honor welling within me will allow me to pursue this courtship any further.

HICKETIER: *(In consternation)* What?

SCHIPPEL: I don't believe so. Got to stick by my decision.

HICKETIER: *(With arms outstretched to him)* Go away, go away! Get out!

SCHIPPEL: *(Steps back)* I get the feeling we won't be in-laws.

(HICKETIER closes in on SCHIPPEL.)

SCHIPPEL: *(Fending him off with an imperious wave of his hand)* Restraint is called for in our embarrassing situation!

(KREY and WOLKE enter.)

SCHIPPEL: At the festival I shall sing like a god!

WOLKE: Whenever I see you without a scarf I fear for your larynx.

KREY: Throat lozenges.

SCHIPPEL: No worries, gentlemen, I know my weighty responsibility as a man of honor.

(HICKETIER is heading for the house.)

SCHIPPEL: Good morning. *Exits.*

WOLKE: (*To* HICKETIER. Listen here!

HICKETIER: *(In the doorway)* Later. *(Exits)*

*(*KREY *pulls* WOLKE *to the elm:)*

KREY: Swear!

WOLKE: I could raise my hand and swear an oath. But first I want to tell you more of what I saw her do: you know the camomile, the delphinium and the dandelion, in short, there isn't a flower that grows that she hasn't plucked as she asks: he loves me—loves me not—loves me!

KREY: Swear, *she* was the one who carved the initials. Swear.

WOLKE: You know the marjoram.

*(*KREY *squeezes* WOLKE *so tight that he squirms.)*

WOLKE: I mean the poison ivy.

KREY: Swear!

*(*KREY *chases* WOLKE, *kicking him in the behind.)*

WOLKE: *(Running)* And it always ended: he loves me…

*(*KREY *has hold of* WOLKE *again and shakes him, roaring, quite beside himself:)*

KREY: An oath! An oath!

WOLKE: What does it matter? *(He raises his hand to swear.)* I swear!

*(*KREY *drops on to a chair and hides his face in his hands.)*

WOLKE: Silly fellow, your kind heart inhibited by prejudice. Look at me, look at your Wolke, who is genuinely fond of you and cannot bear to see your pangs of conscience any longer. But who would also like some peace of mind, Krey. *(With hands raised)* Krey, *(Kneeling before him, shaken with emotion)* take Thekla for your own.

(KREY *raises* WOLKE *up and kisses him:*)

KREY: I can't see the connection, I can't figure out the why and wherefore, when everything was nice and cosy up to now. But your heartfelt tone of voice tells me it has to be. Not another word.

(KREY *and* WOLKE *shake hands.*)

KREY: Wait here; I shall come back engaged. *(Goes into the house)*

WOLKE: There goes a sweet-tempered fellow, graced by God! How can a poor creature such as I compare to him—how does it go?

END OF ACT FOUR

ACT FIVE

(Clearing in a wood. Daybreak)

(The PRINCE *enters right,* THEKLA *left. They run to one another, take hands.)*

PRINCE: You have granted me this last rendezvous, and so my memories of you will ascend to heaven.

THEKLA: I am engaged to the Prince's civil servant Heinrich Krey.

PRINCE: Your brother announced it yesterday at the song festival that ended in triumph for him. Thekla was kept away from me by all sorts of underhanded tricks which offended me as a man of honor. Instead of the anticipated opposition I met with smiles and unlimited acquiescence. Meanwhile you were nowhere to be seen. I came across you only after you had been betrothed. Who was it—who actually dared?

THEKLA: In short, it happened. Had to happen. Even if it's going to cause an imminent death—we're both alive.

PRINCE: *(With a gesture)* Thekla!

THEKLA: You don't mean to seduce me all over again, Highness. You're the man I would gladly belong to, if it were your will. Without you I am just an ordinary girl, God knows. But, as matters stand, I must exercise self-control.

(The PRINCE *moves to put his arm around* THEKLA.*)*

THEKLA: As matters stand, self-control.

PRINCE: Beloved!

THEKLA: *(With one last effort at will power, stamping her feet angrily)* Self-control!

(The PRINCE steps back. THEKLA instantly smiles.)

THEKLA: These last few difficult days, whenever I thought about you and the fate you had in store for me, I had a clearer vision of you than you probably have yourself…

(THEKLA sways. The PRINCE embraces her and holds her for a brief moment, chastely, in his arms.)

THEKLA: You are an enchanting, unforgettable source of happiness for any woman.
Slender, warm and eager as a child, you persuade each of us that she is the first woman you ever embraced, and so deserve her devotion. But you go on accepting the wealth of feelings wasted on you insensibly, with heroic arrogance. Only after many years and many relationships will you understand and trust women. God willing, your image of me will still glow so brightly that I won't be considered unworthy.
(THEKLA takes from her bosom the golden bracelet and gives it to the PRINCE. With tears in her eyes:)
THEKLA: A souvenir of Thekla Hicketier!

(The PRINCE bows deeply over THEKLA's hand.)

THEKLA: Will you escort Heinrich Krey's intended across the fields one last time?

PRINCE: How can you…with him…?

THEKLA: Easily enough. He has displayed a noble character.

PRINCE: *(On the way out)* Promise me that one day you will not say of me: he has displayed a noble character.

Rather, he was an unforgettable source of happiness for women.

THEKLA: My heart agrees to that.

(The PRINCE *and* THEKLA *exit.)*

SCHIPPEL: *(Enters in a tail coat and top hat)* This wretched world brings some situations into clearer focus than any plot summary could. A night full of agonizing anxiety, and a morning that promises not golden dawn but a mouthful of cold death. My generous rejection of the girl, which cost me half my life, and my heroic efforts at the song contest, which, because of me, ended in victory, have earned me nothing but a nod from those sons-of-bitches, and to top it off a challenge to pistols at dawn. All because I hinted to that puffed-up bridegroom that his blushing bride had been playing the field.

How grotesque to be thrust into situations where I have to measure myself by their standards, when I'd prefer any other. Festival yesterday, duel today. I'll never get out of this monkey suit.

But no matter how cleverly you've dug the grave, I won't fall into it. I'll run away! Right now, as far as I can, you're not going to shoot any holes in my ribs. It's murder to demand this of a harmless creature who's never held a firearm in his life. Claiming it's legal. You curs, what was the point of my whole heroic sacrifice, if I can't tell all comers: I jilted Thekla Hicketier—eh?

This is the end of the line, my boy. You've screwed it all up. I would have given an arm and a leg to stay on top. But I simply won't let myself be shot in the belly. For I'm doomed to die, I had awful nightmares, saw myself with a hole as big as a fist in my belly and my guts spilling out.

I've lost everything I held tight in my hands; all I
can save now is my young life. I want to go on flute-
playing and singing, scrounging for tips, so in bed at
night I can feel my body's in one piece, speak my mind
again, not have to constantly keep a leash on the way I
do things.

One short burst of glory when I had Hicketier in
my clutches. But look what it's led to: a corpse lit by
fireworks. Not for this mother's son. Christ almighty!
Blind impulse led me to this spot where I'm supposed
to bite the dust. This is where Krey is to shoot me
down. What I'm doing now is incredibly out of
character, or rather, profoundly appropriate: I'll fade
back into the void from which I came. *(Exits)*

(HICKETIER, KREY *and* WOLKE, *all in tailcoats, enter from
the opposite side.)*

WOLKE: Five minutes to seven. We're the first on the
spot. *(To* KREY*:)* How are you feeling?

HICKETIER: Stop asking him your everlasting questions.
He looks calm enough.

WOLKE: But *my* hair is standing on end. If only I hadn't
finally consented to this unholy duel, if only we had
won Schippel over diplomatically, his future behavior
would be guaranteed. That fellow, I can tell by his
looks, will wield a frightful sword, and skewer Krey
right between the ribs. What's more, in a dream I saw
our friend without a head.

HICKETIER: In my opinion, you've lost yours.

WOLKE: What's taking the Doctor so long? *(To* KREY*:)* Is
your heart pounding? How's your pulse doing? *(Feels
it)* When you took a drink, I saw you've got a coated
tongue. How will this end?

KREY: And things used to be so nice and cosy.

HICKETIER: When the challenge was brought to Schippel, he stood his ground, firm as a rock.

WOLKE: Is that any wonder? He's probably prepared for every bloody eventuality, hasn't had a pistol out of his grip for weeks; whereas I had to explain to Krey for the first time how a trigger works. He's dead meat for such an old hand.

HICKETIER: Don't spoil our conception of this encounter by your cowardice.

WOLKE: I don't give a damn for appearances, the life at stake means more to me than anything on earth.

KREY: *(Pathetically)* Keep quiet, Wolke.

WOLKE: A bridegroom, loving and beloved, at the dawn of his life, is to meet a gruesome death! Isn't there a murder in the offing? Isn't it all your fault, Hicketier? Wasn't it you who informed Krey so graphically of his fiancée's defiled honor, when he, of his own volition, would not have chosen to take violent revenge on a social inferior? Did he not show his generosity when he agreed to throw the veil of love over Thekla's bad behavior? Was it not you who made granting Thekla's hand absolutely dependent on this duel, so that all sorts of incredible things have to happen first? And what for?

(To KREY, *who is on the verge of collapse:)*

WOLKE: Bear up, Krey!
Because in the last analysis you're fascinated by that upstart's machinations. Hicketier, I have long suspected sinister things going on inside you— don't interrupt! Your self-styled superiority is now only a cardboard façade. Heaven has sent Schippel to make your life a misery.

HICKETIER: A pauper, yet he rejected the hundred thousand marks that went with a beautiful girl, and, knowing the miserable fee we'd pay him afterwards, sang us the prize with a divinely unwavering voice. And now, with no experience of challenges, he bravely faces the muzzle of a pistol. The least Krey can do is stand firm in the face of such valor.

WOLKE: People of our sort, conscious of our natural superiority, have no need to compete with Schippel.

KREY: Keep quiet, Wolke.

HICKETIER: I enjoy putting the human qualities of my close friends to the test. Don't undermine Krey at this decisive moment by your pomposity.

WOLKE: Seven o'clock. No one here.

KREY: Maybe he forgot.

HICKETIER: Nonsense! (*He takes a few steps upstage.*)

WOLKE: Two minutes after seven.

KREY: My life was so nice and cosy. And look what you've done to it.

WOLKE: How long do we have to wait actually?

KREY: I feel faint.

HICKETIER: Could they have gone to the wrong place?

WOLKE: Krey is about to have a breakdown.

HICKETIER: (*To* KREY) Ignore Wolke's foolishness.

WOLKE: Eight minutes after seven. Are we obliged to wait here till nightfall?

HICKETIER: They've missed us; we'll have to find them. Come on!

WOLKE: If only there'd be a hurricane, an earthquake!

KREY: My nerves have gone on strike. And life was so nice and cosy.

(WOLKE *takes* KREY *by the arm and almost drags him away.*)

(After a moment MÜLLER *and* SCHULTZE, *dressed in black, enter and wave back. The* DOCTOR, *holding on to* SCHIPPEL's *arm, brings him downstage, where* SCHIPPEL *hides behind a bush, unseen by the others on stage.)*

DOCTOR: Pull yourself together! Don't be a baby.

SCHIPPEL: *(Shaking, in a whisper)* Let me run away, Doctor. If you hadn't just caught me, I'd be over the hills and far away. You're a friend of the poor, let me go!

DOCTOR: Nonsense. The consequences.

SCHIPPEL: Poor people have no consequences.

DOCTOR: Ever since the festival the townsfolk regard you as a celebrity.

SCHIPPEL: A prole, take it from me. Two weeks ago a nobody in a hole. I'll fade back into the night, won't be a bother.

*(*MÜLLER *and* SCHULTZ *have paced out the ground, hammered in stakes. Now they look at their watches.)*

DOCTOR: Your sense of honor, for heaven's sake!

SCHIPPEL: Ah, my dear Doctor, I got none, I swear. Let me go!

DOCTOR: Your opponents will drown you in a flood of ridicule.

SCHIPPEL: Let 'em. That's just what I want, my dear Doctor. I long for it, sheer heaven! I'm just a cur, a miserable wretch— a piece of crap, say it yourself.

DOCTOR: Only a fit of nerves, nothing more.

SCHIPPEL: Certainly not. My knees are knocking. Shaking like a leaf. Death, Doctor! Let me go, Doctor, death! I'll collapse before your very eyes.

*(*HICKETIER, KREY *and* WOLKE *come back.)*

HICKETIER: Here are the gentlemen.

(Bows on all sides)

HICKETIER: The space has been marked out. Each man please to his position.

(Each man goes to his position. KREY and SCHIPPEL stand diagonally opposite one another, so that SCHIPPEL has moved far down right, and KREY occupies the farthest point up left. Next to SCHIPPEL are the DOCTOR, right, and the other two gentlemen, left; by KREY, HICKETIER left, WOLKE right. MÜLLER has taken two pistols out of a case, loaded them, shows them to WOLKE and says:) Two shots each, double barrel. Both loaded.

(WOLKE writhes. The DOCTOR has opened his instrument case. KREY is swaying.)

HICKETIER: *(Quietly to him)* Bear up!

KREY: *(Burbles something like:)* B-lood…

(SCHIPPEL is swaying.)

DOCTOR: *(Quietly to him)* Bear up!

SCHIPPEL: *(Burbles something like:)* D-d-dead.

(SCHULTZE has pulled out a handkerchief to wave like a banner.)

SCHULTZE: *(Counts)* One—two—three!

(And waves the handkerchief. Shots. KREY falls. They all run to him and pull him a few paces offstage.)

DOCTOR: *(Voice)* His arm was grazed. No harm done.

(SCHIPPEL stands alone on stage with outstretched arms like a marble statue, shoots again. Everyone except HICKETIER and WOLKE run to him.)

DOCTOR: Are you crazy? It's all over. Herr Krey has a slight wound. You're untouched.

SCHIPPEL: *(Mechanically)* Thanks.

DOCTOR: Won't you try to make peace with your opponent?

SCHIPPEL: *(Mechanically)* Glad to.

(SCHIPPEL lets the DOCTOR take him upstage.)

WOLKE: *(Steps out to meet him)* You have my thanks, you noble, noble-minded man. Wolke will never forget your magnanimity.

HICKETIER: *(Comes and says to MÜLLER and SCHULTZE)* Your party's bearing was heroic.

(MÜLLER and SCHULTZE bow.)

HICKETIER: Filled with the same serenity and confidence he showed at the song festival.

(MÜLLER and SCHULTZE bow.)

HICKETIER: What an honor to serve as seconds to such a marksman.

(MÜLLER and SCHULTZE bow. They exit. SCHIPPEL comes back. HICKETIER walks up to him. Both men, alone on stage, exchange a look. HICKETIER says:)

HICKETIER: Hate-filled prejudice and a stubborn aversion to your origins kept me from admitting you to our circle. You have bested me. I consider it my duty to declare how honored your company shall make me in future.

(HICKETIER holds out both his hands to SCHIPPEL.)

SCHIPPEL: Glad to hear it.

HICKETIER: This day will have consequences. The memory of what you have achieved must not be forgotten, and I take it on myself personally to see that the lofty blessings of middle-class life be granted to you in full. See you soon, my dear Herr Schippel. *(He tips his hat respectfully to him. Exit)*

SCHIPPEL: *(Alone in full blazing sunlight, deeply overcome, hides his face in his hands)* Their blessings in full—it's too much. *(Quietly, blissfully happy)* At last, Paul, you're a bourgeois. *(He makes a sweeping bow to himself.)*

END OF PLAY

www.ingramcontent.com/pod-product-compliance
Lightning Source LLC
Chambersburg PA
CBHW070025110426
42741CB00034B/2534